FULLNESS!

Living Beyond Revivals and Outpourings

by

Rick Manis

FULLNESS!

Living Beyond Revivals and Outpourings

by

Rick Manis

Empyrion Publishing

Winter Garden FL 34778

EmpyrionPublishing.com

Empyrion Publishing

Winter Garden FL 34778

EmpyrionPublishing.com

Unless otherwise noted, all Scripture quotations are from the King James Version of the Bible.

Printed in the United States of America

To my late wife, Teresa:

Thank you for your love and support.
Together, we made an incredible team.

Acknowledgements

Thanks to the many brothers and sisters in the Lord who encouraged me to write a book, much to my resistance. You are too numerous to name, but you know who you are. You encouraged me in our conversations as I have ministered in my travels.

Special thanks to my late wife, Teresa, who convinced me that it was the will of God. What a partner she was!

Mostly, to the Holy Spirit who faithfully led me and taught me in a way I could never have known on my own. He showed me things I wasn't even looking for. He truly is the real author and inspiration of this book.

Contents

Introduction

The body of Christ has completed an important season. In that season the key words were *hunger, thirst, passion, seeking, pursuing, preparation, purging,* and *process*.

We are now in a new day! The key words for this time are *fullness, wholeness, completeness,* and *satisfaction*.

This reformation is better than any revival, or outpouring, or touch of God. It is better than any glimpse of glory or visitation. The Lord is offering us an elevated walk with Him in His world!

I have written this book to help those who are hungry and thirsty for righteousness to complete the transition from the highs and lows of the past season, and into the consistent, glory filled life you have been promised.

This book is essentially about deliverance from the root of all of our problems, namely, lust.

However, before you close the book and put it down let me pique your interest. There is no reference to sexual sin in these pages, nor is gluttony mentioned.

While those who struggle with the aforementioned will find their answer in these writings, I wish to deal with kind of lust that may plague even the cleanest living of Christians.

It's the lust of good things and holy things that keep us from the next level. It could even be the lust for God.

I've heard it said that the only good lust is a lust for God, but lust is lust no matter what its object is, and lust by its nature can never be filled or satisfied. It is a sense of need, hunger, thirst, desire, passion, want, or lack.

Still, lust is not defeated just because the church tells us it's wrong. You can't will it to stop. The only way to stop lusting, or hungering; is to be full. Fullness is the answer!

That is why the Lord is bringing us out of our hungry season and into the time of fullness.

As a minister of the Lord for many years, I have gone through many seasons. I became adept at spiritual warfare, as well as groaning and travail. I have fasted and prayed more than anyone I know. I know firsthand about the testing of the wilderness, and have poured out my soul like water in brokenness and humility.

Then I came to a new season. It has been like a perpetual springtime. The spiritual exercises that once consumed me and defined me are not found here. There is too much abundance here to be needy or desperate.

This is my attempt to reveal what I see prophetically, what I am experiencing vitally, and what the Bible says about these things.

I believe I present a perspective that doesn't have a loud enough voice yet. I believe it is to us a new sound, declaring new things that are springing forth. Let us all go into the time of fullness.

"My people shall be satisfied with my goodness, saith the Lord."

Jeremiah 31:14

Chapter 1

Father I Quit

"Blessed are they which do hunger and thirst after righteousness, for they shall be filled."
Matthew 5:6

Father, I'm sorry for letting you down. I know you had plans for me. I know that you wanted me to walk in your glory, but I can't get there. I'm not strong enough, and I don't have what it takes. I can't try any more. Father, I quit."

Those were the words of my prayer as I lay on my back, looking toward Heaven with tears in my eyes. This was my formal resignation as a seeker of God.

I still loved Him, and I didn't want to sever our relationship, but I was tired of all of the spiritual labor involved in pressing on to the high call. I was done.

I didn't know what the consequence of my prayer would be. Would I be doomed to the spiritual complacency that I despised? Should I now quit the ministry? Would God's presence depart from me? Would I ever hear His voice again?

Up until this time, when it came to passion and zeal I was a top model. I was usually the last to leave a prayer meeting, and I usually shouted the loudest, worshipped the deepest, and fasted more often than those around me.

As a minister, I had a reputation for stirring that type of passion and creating that kind of seeker. Complacency was intimidated in my presence. I was committed to bombarding the gates of glory unto holiness and power.

At times I *would* experience the overwhelming presence of God. It was so perfect, so clean, so powerful, and so right; but I could never maintain it. When the time of refreshing was over I was back to being me. So I went to work seeking my next breakthrough. Years of repeating that same cycle left me somewhat better than where I started. I experienced many blessings, and learned a lot of things, but I simply was not satisfied with where it left me, and I still seemed light years from knowing God the way I wanted to.

So there I was. My unfinished journey aborted. Then it happened…

As I lay defeated on that floor, I felt the heavens open. God's glory and fullness overflowed me, and I sensed the biggest smile of God that you could imagine. I heard Him say, "Good. Are you done now?"

While lying on that floor, the Lord began to give me a revelation. It was a real fullness that was not based on a feeling or an event. It was truly the end of my seeking, and It would finally quench my desire. It would change my life, no, the world!

It was so powerful and so earth shaking. The pillars of my temple began to crumble. I was crushed in the destruction, yet it felt great! I was being liberated from my own destructions. I gladly lay prone. The loss I was experiencing was actually giving me room to breathe. In being humbled, I became large. In losing my world, I was receiving Heaven.

Truth came in to sup with me that day and He never left. I knew I could now go on. God didn't need my strength. He was enough. He was everything, and I had Him. That day I began to know, and grow in the revelation of fullness.

Your Wilderness Season Has Come to an End

Not long after that, I heard the Holy Spirit speak to me these words: "Your wilderness season has come to an end. I will now take your life and lift it up as a trophy of my goodness and a showcase of my glory. People will look at you and know that I am good".

You would have thought that I would rejoice and shout "hallelujah" at hearing such great news, but no. Though my wilderness season had seemed overly elongated and had been extremely hard, it was also the sweetest time of my life. I had become passionate for God in that season of hunger. I had been set free from so many things. I cherished the intimacy I had found in that time of seeking. It didn't come easy. It came through hardships, trial, and the pouring out of self toward nothingness. It was precious, and I didn't want to trade it for anything.

Not only that, but I still didn't look finished. I still had too much carnality about me. I wasn't Christ-like in all of my actions. Why abandon my inward growth process after I've come so far? I begged the Lord to finish the work before He brought me out of the wilderness and into the land of milk and honey.

He then gave me this assurance: "I didn't say that your growth had come to an end. You have been learning through trials, suffering and hardship; but you will now learn by my favor, goodness and blessing".

Then I realized that I was about to learn of Him in ways I could never know in the desert. I was about to come into the next season of my life, a final perpetual season. I was about to live in fullness!

No More Roller Coaster Ride

I soon began to noticeably experience more favor and joy. It was what I call a "mountain top" experience, where you are aware of God's presence and good things are happening to you.

I'd had many of these times in my Christian walk in the past, but they never lasted very long. They were always followed by a "valley" experience. So over the years, I learned to milk these "highs" for everything they were worth, knowing they could never last. Times of abundance were always followed by a time of scarcity. Times of glory that could make you laugh, cry, and knock you off of your feet were always followed by another time of hunger and seeking the next high.

But this time it was different. Weeks had passed, and no valley yet. I often found myself wondering when the rug would be pulled out from under me. Every time I thought that, the Holy Spirit would remind me that it's a new season.

Every good thing in my life began to increase. My marriage was happier. My ministry was more fruitful. Financially, I began to experience more than enough instead of barely enough or rarely enough.

Spiritually, I found that my love and gratitude toward God had a natural authentic flow. I was more aware of His presence than ever before, and I didn't have to "enter in". I just seemed to be walking under an open heaven. I wasn't asking for anything, because all I touched was beginning to prosper, so my prayer life had no ritual at all. It was just a real love and appreciation that constantly flowed from my heart.

Over time, I realized that this was a season that God was bringing a generation into. It was the season of fullness, and it would never end. We were a people that the prophets of old spoke of. We were those who would live from mountain top to mountain top, from glory to glory, from faith to faith.

He Brought You *Through*, To Get You *To...*

Have you been promised a walk in God's world? Have you always known that God has more for you than you've been experiencing? Have you had a sense that you were a part of the generation that would carry God's glory like no other generation has? Have you been holding to a promise of healing, restoration, or other great blessing?

God has not cast His pearls before swine! He did not show you those things only to tease you with something you will never have. He did not bring you through all the hell you've been through, just to get you through more hell in the future. No, He brought you *through* to get you *to* this wonderful day!

It's here! You made it! This is the day of the Lord! It's your appointed time! God told you it would come. Why not now?

There will be no more waiting for it. No more of the "old school" preparation, purging, or process. No more hunger, thirst, or want. No more rehearsing. On with the show, this is it!

The calendar has changed. You have been brought to the kingdom for such a time as this.

You have been called and prepared to walk in fullness. You are about to experience what your heart desires, and what your heart desires... is to stop desiring.

Fullness!

Chapter 2

The Nature of Lust

"Whereby are given to us exceeding great and precious promises; that by these ye might be partakers of the divine nature, having escaped the corruption that is in this world through lust."

II Peter 1:4

Look up the definition of lust. You will find that it doesn't necessarily have to do with sexual things. Lust is a desire, hunger, thirst, or sense of need. It comes from a perceived lack of something.

According to the above verse, lust is the vehicle that brought all of the death and destruction that is in this world. It is truly the original sin.

Most people think that the original sin was rebellion, or treason, or pride, or ambition; but the original sin was lust.

Fullness!

Adam disobeyed God, but before he committed the act of disobedience he had an inner problem that caused the outward action.

"But every man is tempted when he is drawn away of his own lust and enticed"

James 4:14.

What was the bait that the snake used to get us to eat of the tree of knowledge of good and evil? What could possibly entice us to commit such a transgression? What was it we were lusting for? What was the thing we longed for, thirsted for, hungered for? What did we earnestly desire? In what area were we not satisfied?

"...ye shall be as gods, knowing good and evil"

Genesis 3:5

We wanted to be like God. We still do. It's not a bad thing.

Have you ever prayed that you could love as He does, see as He does, walk as He does? Isn't your goal to be as much like the Lord as you can be? It's not a bad thing.

So when Adam and Eve ate of that tree, they weren't trying to do something bad. They were going after something good. They weren't out to commit treason. They were trying to fill a hunger for Godliness. They simply wanted to be like Him, to commune with Him and walk with Him on His level.

But they did do the wrong thing. They did commit sin. They did bring the fall of man.

A lot of people today think that Adam's problem was weakness. They wish man had just said "no" to the serpent. They are the ones who think that weakness is our problem today. They are always trying to become strong, thinking that strength is the antidote to their spiritual shortcomings.

Others think Adam and Eve should have had more passion for God so they could have resisted the temptation. They think revival is the answer today, because revival stirs up zeal.

Man's problem was not weakness, lack of zeal, or a wrong motive. It was ignorance. It still is. Where there is lust, or lack, or need, or hunger; you will always find ignorance.

"My people are destroyed for lack of knowledge..."
Hosea 4:6

Our destruction came because we didn't know something. We didn't know who we were. Most of us still don't.

Remember, when God made us He created us in His likeness and in His image. If we were created in His likeness, then why did we feel the need to do something else to become like Him?

Man should have told the serpent, "I'm already like Him! I was created in His likeness! I don't have to eat from a tree or do any religious exercise to be like Him. I am who I am by virtue of the I Am who created me, and I am Junior!"

"... as He is, so are we in this world"

I John 4:17.

However, the man did not do that. He (male and female) ate of the tree, trying to become what he already was, trying to get what he already had. Many of us still do.

Adam was not aware of who he was. He had a perceived lack, a need, a hunger, a desire (lust).

Lust is never satisfied. It perpetuates a sense of need and creates more desire for its object.

That's why the more I pursued the Lord the more I hungered for Him. The more water I drank, the more I thirsted for it. I even taught others that this was the way it was supposed to be. We are so good at canonizing our experience.

"But whosoever drinketh of the water that I shall give him, shall never thirst..."

John 4:14

The hungry and thirsty are supposed to be *filled*, not continue to hunger and thirst. God promised that He would *satisfy* our soul.

The only thing that will make us free is the *truth*, which is the revelation of Jesus Christ.

"And ye are complete in Him..."

Colossians 2:10

The revelation of Jesus Christ crucifies the incomplete mindset. It causes us to live the life we live by the faith of the Son of God.

The First Adam - The Last Adam

The first man lusted after that which he already had. His sense of inferiority caused a **rest**-lessness, resulting in spiritual striving.

In Luke 2:22 we witness the baptism of Jesus, with the Father's voice declaring, *"Thou art my beloved Son, in thee I am well pleased"*.

Then He leaves the Jordan River to be tested by the devil.

What is interesting is that the writer interrupts the story to list the genealogy of Jesus. Luke traces it back to Adam, calling Adam the *son of God*.

Watch this! Jesus was just announced at the river as the Son of God. Luke announces that Adam also was the son of God. Both sons, one fallen, another standing. The one standing would now be tested in the same way as the first one, but this one would pass the test, and where the first man was destroyed for a lack of knowledge, the last Adam would restore us through an abundance of knowledge!

"...by his knowledge shall my righteous servant justify many..."

Isaiah 53:11

The last Adam, Jesus, had a sense of fullness and completeness. When He was tested in the same way as man was before, Jesus didn't bite the bait. He knew who He was!

The accuser challenged Him on His sonship, but to no avail. Jesus had nothing to prove to the Father, or to himself, or to some devil.

He would not have to turn rocks into bread, or do a swan dive from the roof of the church, or be forced into worship. He already had the Father's approval, and no religious exercise would add to it. He needed to do nothing to become anything, because He was God's son, period.

"Beloved, now are we the sons of God..."

I John 3:2.

Notice that Jesus was approved *before* He was tested. Before He passed or failed, He was already a beloved son.

What about you? Are you trying to gain the Father's approval, His blessing, His favor?

Are you jumping through hoops in order to get Him to bless you?

Are you trying to find some missing act of obedience that's keeping you from enjoying the fullness of God?

The approval of the Father empowers the sons!

Eating of the tree of knowledge of good and evil (knowing right and wrong) is not the answer. Entering into rest is the answer.

Before you do another good act, you are already approved by God. Because you are approved, you have all that you will ever need. You are all you ever need to be.

When you really know that, you know that you don't have to worship and praise the Lord in order to be blessed. You worship and praise *because* you are blessed!

You don't have to give tithes and offerings to be blessed. You give them *because* you are blessed!

Fullness!

You don't have to pray so that God will bless you. You commune with Him often *because* He has blessed you!

Those who walk after the order of the first man are needy. As long as there is need, there will be lust. The only way to overcome lust is to be truly full, satisfied, and complete in Him.

The church needs to be delivered of the sin and error of lusting after God.

"...My people will be satisfied with My goodness, saith the Lord."

Jeremiah 31:14

Chapter 3

Why We Lust After God

"There is a way which seemeth right unto a man, but the end thereof are the ways of death."

Proverbs 16:25

First, let me state that our lust for God has to stop. I did not say that our (desire) for God was wrong, in fact, it takes a pure motive of the heart to want God in that way. However, lusting for God is born out of the same ignorance as lust for anything else. It all comes from a sense of lack or need.

I've heard Christians say that the only good lust is a lust for God, but all they are doing is redirecting the desire that they once had for other things.

It sounds good doesn't it? But was that desire, when it was turned toward other things, ever satisfied by its object?

Fullness!

No, because lust by its nature can never satisfy. The belly never stays full. The novelty of new things wears off quickly. The millionaire needs more money.

Lust can only be pacified temporarily, and no matter how much our desire is catered to, we are eventually left feeling just as hungry as before.

It is because we approach God with this spirit of longing that we have extreme highs and lows in our walk with Him. Like spiritual drug addicts, we pursue the "Most High". Occasionally we score. During this time our serotonin and adrenaline levels rise. We are energized, uninhibited and unselfish. We feel strong and elevated.

I will say that I enjoy times of personal and corporate revival as much as anyone! Give me a lively church service over a dead one any day. I can party in the spirit with the best of them.

But what I don't like is the inconsistency. I don't like that the same believer who is energized, uninhibited, unselfish, strong and elevated during these times of refreshing will again become weary, self-conscious and needy.

Lusting after God produces a cycle of highs and lows, creating more want instead of less want. Lust is never satisfied.

"...The Lord is my shepherd; I shall not want."

Psalms 23:1

I will now show you four reasons why God's children lust after Him.

Reason #1 – Old Testament Glory

Throughout the Old Testament, the hunger of holy men and prophets is painfully expressed. Their cries of desperation stir our own passion. We who also hunger for God can feel their pain. We know exactly what they were talking about.

Or do we?

I honestly believe that those Old Testament saints who surround us as witnesses are marveling that we can't see the truth under our nose. Perhaps they are amazed that we are still seeking what they diligently looked for.

They cried out to know Him. They desired to be with Him. They hungered for holiness. They thirsted for righteousness.

Jesus had not come yet. The new creation had not been born. The veil between Heaven and Earth had not been ripped, but now it has! Behold, all things have become new! It's not the same as it used to be! How can we even relate to the Old Testament cries of the impoverished first man? We are of the new order! We are complete in Him!

Yet our worship songs continue to echo the destitute hearts of incomplete men. We sing of our desperation for God, pulling our lyrics from the low level religion of an inferior, outdated condition.

A pastor once told me, "Now I know why the Bible tells us to 'sing a new song', it's because you ruin all of our old ones!"

Reason #2 – We Think it's a High Place

I'm going to say something that I hope is not too offensive to consider. I have noticed that there is a certain element of the spirit of pride in those who overly exalt the hungering and thirsting for God. I certainly noticed it in myself.

I felt that we who were voraciously pursuing God were a cut above other Christians. I spoke condescendingly of those who could not be brought to tears and cries of passion. I knew that nobody could out-hunger me, and that set me a little higher than they. Surely my heart was purer than my peers, for I fasted more, prayed longer, and wept more openly in brokenness and humility. I reveled in humility, because others wanted it and I had it. Yeah, right.

We think that our spiritual longing is the beat all to end all. We think it's the most holy and pure condition that our heart can attain. We set it as the goal for all serious believers.

But hunger is not the goal! It is only a means to an end. It's not a condition that one should aspire to. It's a condition that one should come out of!

"Blessed are they which do hunger and thirst after righteousness, for they shall be filled."

Matthew 5:6

They shall be *filled*, not keep on hungering. We have focused on the *hungering and thirsting* rather than the *filling*. That is typical for the mind that still relates more to the fallen nature instead of the risen.

We think longing is the height of spirituality, but the height of spirituality is being filled!

But why do so many that thirst, continue to thirst even though they drink often? It's because they are stuck. What is supposed to be a temporary season has become perpetual. It has become their place of familiarity. It has become home.

They need to be willing to leave that high maintenance home, that handyman special, for a fully functional mansion. That is the purpose for this book. I want to give you permission to leave that season behind, and move into fullness. It is the will of God.

Your hunger should take you to a revelation, not a revival, for with this revelation of fullness you will never need revival again.

Reason #3 – Ignorance of Fullness

Look at the following verse of scripture. Is it telling us to seek the Lord?

"...it is time to seek the Lord, till He come and rain righteousness upon you."

Hosea 10:12

Most would say so, but notice the word, "till". It means that our seeking should come to an end at some time.

When is that time? Is it when a revival hits, or we get high on the Spirit again? What is the rain of righteousness?

The rain of righteousness is the *reign* of righteousness! It is this wonderful day that we live in, when Jesus became sin for us, that we would be made the righteousness of God in Him.

Both theologically and chronologically, God has rained righteousness all over us, and His glory is here like the waters cover the sea. It's been here for two-thousand years, but the church's needy mindset continues to put it off into the future. The church doesn't *need* the glory of God. It's here! What they are missing is the *knowledge* of the glory.

*"For the earth shall be filled with the **knowledge** of the glory of the Lord, as the waters cover the sea."*

Habakkuk 2:14

God is here! Why seek Him? He lives within you. How much closer does He need to be?

What are we looking for? What are waiting for? We are supposed to be preaching good news. The good news is that the kingdom is at hand. That means it is here, now! Bad news is that you have to wait on it, work for it, and do without it for a while.

I do understand that that we need to hunger and seek if we know we need something that we are just not experiencing, but I am also telling you what brings an end to your hunger and lust. It is the knowledge of how great your salvation really is!

It's like someone with a full plate of food begging for more. They don't know what they have, so they go around hungry, always asking for more.

You will never have more of God than you do now, but you will have more knowledge, clarity, and awareness of the Greater One in you. The secret that's been hid from the ages, but is now being revealed is Christ in you, the hope of glory.

Fullness!

"That the communication of your faith may become effectual by the acknowledging of every good thing which is in you in Christ Jesus."

Philemon 1:6

Reason #4 – Spiritual Carnality

One aspect of carnality is sense-mindedness. That is, being more in tune with temporary things than eternal. So, spiritual carnality would be a temporary spirituality. It is based on our outward senses.

In this low level of spirituality, God is in the house if we feel Him. We wait on God to heal us, thinking that until we see physical proof, He has done nothing. Because we don't see the outward proof of the fullness of God (a proof that our mind demands), we lust for it, wait for it, pray for it to come.

"And when He was demanded of the Pharisees when the kingdom of God should come, He answered them and said, The kingdom of God cometh not with observation. Neither shall they say, Lo here, or, Lo there, for, behold, the kingdom of God is within you."

Luke 17:20-21

We do have wonderful times of refreshing in that low level of spiritual carnality. It seems that our seeking is rewarded by outpourings and touches and visitations; but why should we continually settle for these temporary experiences when we can have it eternally now?

I will never again have to "enter in" to the Spirit of God. I wake up every morning knowing I am under an open heaven. I will never need to break through the veil. Jesus already did that for me. My labor and waiting has ceased. Now I can freely receive, and freely give.

I am not saying we have to give up the wonderful feelings we have had in our other seasons. I'm saying you can now have it all of the time! God is not calling us to another experience. He is showing us an elevated walk in His world.

I don't chase spiritual "highs" anymore, because my "high" is now more consistent. Revivals only excite me because of their impact on hungry humanity, which I am not a part of, so it adds little to me personally.

God wants us to know the truth that will make us free. The truth is that we are not needy! We have God and He is enough. We need nothing. When we know this truth, it breaks all of our religious addictions and lusts.

This is the next level, and it is where you go when you're ready to go beyond revivals, outpourings, and moves of God.

Fullness!

Chapter 4

Why We Lust After Revival

*"...I caused it to rain upon one city, and caused it not to rain upon another city... so two or three cities wandered into one city, to drink water, **but they were not satisfied...**"*

Amos 4:7-8.

Let me say first of all, that revivals are wonderful. They are refreshing, animated, fun, powerful and glorious! I have enjoyed many such times of refreshing in my own local church, as well as some historic, documented moves of God in the body of Christ. Revivals kindle the fire of passion, bringing joy and demonstrations of power to the church.

But why does every revival have to end? Why do they always fade away? Why, after thousands of years of such movements in the church do we still need yet another one? Why are some of the ministries that hosted recent revivals worse off now than before the move started?

Old vs. New Covenant Glories

The answer lies in the nature of revival itself. Though we live in a New Testament time, we may still be partaking of outdated, Old Testament glories.

If the revival fades away, it is because it is temporary by nature and will never satisfy. When it ends, we are ready to get down and start praying for the next one…again.

Eventually, another revival will come with another leader who will be our hero for the day. We will come from afar to partake of his anointing. Our needy, inferior souls will want to be like him. We will line up to be touched by this hand of God. We dare not miss out on such a gem of a movement.

Later, the revival will fade. Too often they end in scandal, strife or impropriety. So we pray for the next one…again.

But do not despair! There is a revival unlike any other. It is a reviving that comes from revealed knowledge. It does not fade. It is not hungry or needy. It is simply a revelation of fullness.

Revelation means "uncovering". It is not the creating of something new. It is the uncovering of something that has always been there. You've had it the whole time. Now it's time to enjoy it!

This "last" move, if you will, is a glory that will not fade, but burn brighter and brighter. It is the progressive unveiling of the fullness of Christ in you! It is an ever increasing knowledge. It takes you from glory to glory, from faith to faith, from mountain top to mountain top; not from peak to valley over and over again.

I've had many mountain top experiences over the years, but they never lasted. My roller coaster experience with God trained me to not expect the good times to last. When things were going well, I learned to milk the season for all I could, because I knew it had to end. Sure enough, it did.

God is offering something better than a revival, or an outpouring, or a visitation, or a glimpse of glory, or any religious spasm. He is offering something better than an experience. He is offering an elevation!

There will still be revivals, and they will bless a lot of people, but there are more and more of us who have moved on to the next level. We have a sense of completeness and wholeness. God satisfies our souls. Our cups run over! We hunger and thirst no more. We are partaking of the new covenant glory, the glory that does not fade. Revivals always fade, and that is the mark of the Old Testament glory.

I used to pray for an experience like Solomon had when God's glory filled the house so that the priests could not stand to minister. God answered that prayer many times. I recall meetings that I held where people just fell out, slain in the Spirit during the worship or preaching without any suggestions. Still I was not satisfied, and only thirsted more.

I used to want what Moses got when he prayed on the mountain that God would show him His glory. I marveled that the face of Moses shone so brightly. Surely this was the kind of manifested glory that the church needs.

But again, it was a glory that could not remain. It faded.

"But if the ministry of death... was glorious, so that the children of Israel could not look at the face of Moses... which glory was (fading) away, how will the ministry of the Spirit not be more glorious?... For if what (fades) away was glorious, what remains is much more glorious.

II Corinthians 3:7-11 NKJV

We should not be jealous of Solomon, or Moses, or any of the prophets. They would have loved to have what we have!

"...many prophets and righteous men have desired to see those things which ye see, and have not..."

Matthew 13:17.

Pray For Rain, Or Drink From The Fountain?

Hungry believers are always seeking a spiritual rain or outpouring. Their external mindset wants the anointing to "fall". They want God to "pour out" His blessings.

The thing about rain is, you always need another one. It never satisfies. It refreshes wonderfully, but never satisfies. God has promised to give times of refreshing, but He also has promised to satisfy.

*"And I will **pour** upon the house of David... the spirit of grace and of supplications... and they shall mourn..."*

Zechariah 12:10.

*"In that day there shall be a **fountain** opened to the house of David... for sin and for uncleanness. And it shall come to pass... that I will cut off the names of*

the idols out of the land, and they shall no more be remembered..."

Zechariah 13:1-2.

In the outpourings, we experience grace and supplications, or favor and fervent prayer. However, the mourning doesn't end.

But He also said He would open a fountain, the Spirit within us. It would be this inner anointing that would rid us of sin, uncleanness and idolatry.

Have you noticed that outpourings don't rid us of those things? In fact, many revivals of recent notoriety have had church splits, and sometimes the revival leaders themselves become involved in sin.

Are they real revivals? Yes they are, but revival only provides favor and fervor. They do not bring wholeness. Only the fountain within you can do that.

The fountain of living water destroys lust, because it makes us complete, not needy.

The fountain destroys idolatry, which is the bowing of our knees to things other than God. The power within us is greater than habits, sickness, circumstances, even death.

The trap of revival is that it is so refreshing that we become addicted to it, keeping us looking to the sky instead of within the temple. The temporal season has so many heavenly manifestations, so we think we need revivals in order to have these manifestations.

Ministries get trapped in revival because so many people become dependent on their gift. As long as there is a large "subclass" of Christians, revival will be the focus of our ministries, books, prophecies, and conferences.

"...they have forsaken me the fountain of living waters, and hewed them out cisterns, broken cisterns, that can hold no water."

Jeremiah 2:13

While the church is looking for an outpouring, creation is looking for the manifestation of the sons of God (Rom. 8:19).

While the church is looking for an event, the world is looking for you!

When the Son came, John the Baptist was looking for Him. There was one way John would know who He was.

*"And John bare record saying, I saw the Spirit descending from Heaven like a dove, and it (stayed) upon Him. And I knew Him not, but He who sent me... said unto me, Upon whom thou shalt see the Spirit descending, and **remaining** on Him... And I saw and bare record that this is the Son of God."*

John 1:32-34

Fullness!

The way that the *Son* was recognized is the same way the *sons* are recognized, the Spirit *remains*. It doesn't come and go.

In the days of Noah, after the rain stopped, he sent a dove out into the earth. Not finding a resting place, it kept coming back to him. Finally, when the dove found a place to call home, it remained in the earth, and didn't return.

That's the different between the Old Testament glory and the New Testament glory. It never leaves us!

It never leaves because it is based on truth, not emotional ties to events. Jesus said the truth will make us free, not events. We are changed by a renewed mind, not an event.

In my meetings, events do happen. There are instant healings, people are slain in the Spirit, and many times a revival atmosphere is evident, but I've been around long enough to know that none of these things alone can bring freedom. We have to think and see things on a level we've not know before.

"Wisdom is the principal thing, therefore get wisdom: and with all thy getting get understanding"

Proverbs 4:7

Those who walk in the sonship level of their inheritance are enjoying a consistently heavenly

~ 34 ~

existence. They are not up then down, refreshed then dry, joyful then depressed, anointed then not anointed, in the Spirit then out. They don't need a touch. They *are* a touch. They don't need a word. They *are* a word. They don't need an outpouring. They *are* an outpouring. They don't need a revival they *are* a revival.

Christians must break out of the needy mindset. Until they do, they will feel that they need more than they already have. Because they don't know what we already possess, they beg, strive, and bombard heaven trying to receive from God.

Why do we always need to be refilled?

Jesus taught us that old wineskins cannot hold new wine. The new wine will always leak out.

Your wineskin is your mindset, doctrine, or belief system.

There are powerful messages being heard in this hour, yet the hearers struggle to make it their everyday life. There are powerful events happening in the church today, yet those who partake of it can't seem to maintain that high experience. The wine runs out, and they must get filled again and again.

They leak. Their mindset is still in the old cycle, so the old patterns keep repeating, and little, if any progress is made.

I have seen people throw their crutches away and dance in my meetings. Some were on crutches again within weeks. When they were removed from the atmosphere of the event, they couldn't stand against the pressure of fallen creation.

I know of many that were delivered from habits, they rejoiced in their new holiness, abstaining for weeks only to return to the habit again. The thought patterns that caused their bondage initially were still in place, and eventually overcame them. The preacher's touch was not enough.

The new wineskin is a mindset of fullness. The renewed mind says God has given us all we need. It's a mindset that knows we have it now. It's a way of thinking that can keep and carry the fullness of God!

When Jesus taught about the wineskins, He was answering a question from the disciples of John the Baptist. They wanted to know why they fasted often, but the disciples of Jesus never did.

The answer is that you don't mourn when things are great! Jesus was with them. Restoration was happening. Truth was being heard. Needs were being met. Why should they interrupt all of that with fasting and seeking?

Though John the Baptist was the greatest prophet of the old order, his movement was not a move of fullness. It pointed forward, looking toward fullness. It's interesting that even after John told the people to follow Jesus, many still followed John. You can live in the day of milk and honey, but still scratch for manna if you don't know the times and seasons.

As long as Jesus was with them, there was no need for religious calisthenics.

He is with us today, and will never leave us. If you don't know that, you will keep looking.

"And when He was demanded of the Pharisees, when the kingdom of God should come, He answered them and said, The kingdom of God cometh not with observation: Neither shall they say, Lo here! or, Lo there! For behold, the kingdom of God is within you. ... And they shall say to you, See here! Or, See there; go not after them nor follow them"

Luke 17:20-23

The new wineskin is a mindset that is aware of the glory within, rather than looking for the glory to be poured upon us. The new man doesn't invite the Holy Spirit, but acknowledges His indwelling presence.

God does give outpourings to those who want them, but we with new wineskins have moved beyond want. We enjoy the rain with everyone else, but if it doesn't rain, we drink from the river that never runs dry!

Fullness!

Chapter 5

Why We Lust After Things

"...for your heavenly Father knoweth that you have need of all these things. But seek ye first the kingdom of God, and His righteousness, and all these things shall be added unto you."

Matthew 6:32-33

Again, we pursue what we think we lack. God's word tells us not to be anxious for things because He knows that we need them.

He didn't say we should just learn to live without them. He didn't say that things weren't important. They are. He said we need them, but He also doesn't want us to lust after them.

We shouldn't lust after them because lust is never satisfied. It doesn't matter how abundant or how little your accumulation is, you will never feel good about it.

God wants you to be satisfied.

Almost invariably, when I make that statement in my meetings, the crowd gets quiet and looks confused. They mistake satisfaction for complacency and settling for less, but to be satisfied means to be satiated, saturated or soaked. It means to be so full that there is no more room. It's fullness!

God knows that we need things. Some are necessary to survive in this human experience. Others enable and empower us to do more good. Still other things are simply for us to enjoy.

"...God, who giveth us richly all things to enjoy."
I Timothy 6:17

You don't have to draw the line of limitation anywhere. There is more than enough for everybody! God has created a wonderful world full of wonderful things. He made them for us!

We are spirit beings in a human, earthy experience. We rightly operate in both the visible and invisible realm. We are to partake of both worlds in a way so that Heaven and Earth come together in our life. The best is to fully partake of both without harming either side.

For example, it's obvious that you can indulge in things of this earth that hinder your spirituality. You can also be spiritually indulgent in a way that neglects earthly functions, so that you are no earthly good.

But there is a way to enjoy fullness in both worlds. You have to know that you already have everything!

"...His divine power has given unto us all things that pertain unto life and godliness..."

II Peter 1:3

If you already have it, how can you lust after it? Knowing you have it is called *faith*, and faith brings it into manifestation!

When it looks like my bills are bigger than my income, I look around with my spirit eyes, and all I see is wealth and riches. I don't feel needy or lacking. I feel rich, not anxious. Anxiety or feelings of despair and need will only make it worse. Feeling rich makes money come, always! When you know that you have your inheritance, which is the kingdom of God, then you know you have everything. God said all these things are then added to you. Abundance inside produces abundance outside!

Some people think I have a lust for things, because I believe in having abundance in this world, but the truth is, I don't lust after them because I think I already have them.

This way, I can go after my God-given dreams without being anxious or frustrated at any time. I never wonder if it will happen. It's only a matter of when and how. These are two issues I'm not overly concerned with because my sense of abundance gives me perfect peace about it.

It's the perfect combination of contentment and expectancy.

Why Do Some Ungodly Folks Have So Much?

Some have gotten riches and things without seeking first the kingdom of God. If so, then they are just poor people with money. Again, they find that it is never enough. They are driven by lust.

To so many people, success is a way of trying to make an unfulfilled soul feel worthy. It's a way of gaining respect for a soul that feels disrespected. It's a way of feeling rich for a soul that feels and fears poverty. They always feel lacking, that's why they love and need to be treated as one in a higher class than most. Often smug and proud, they continue to pour success into a hole called lust that can never be filled.

They *trust* in riches. Jesus never said that wealth was bad, but if you *trust* in riches you will never be satisfied.

"I can't get no satisfaction. 'Cause I try and I try, and I try, and I try..."
Mick Jagger, Keith Richards – The Rolling Stones

Worldly Success:	**Godly Success:**
Driven by *want*.	Motivated by *already having*.
Striving for greatness.	*Created* by greatness.
Doesn't satisfy the soul.	Comes from a satisfied soul.
Raises your status in life.	Raises other people's status.
Can add sorrow.	Adds no sorrow

"The blessing of the Lord, it maketh rich, and He addeth no sorrow with it."

Proverbs 10:22

Fullness!

Chapter 6

Why We Lust After Greatness

"And seekest thou great things for thyself? Seek them not..."

Jeremiah 45:5

Most people, even Christians struggle with the battle against selfishness, self-consciousness, and self-centeredness. Because they live like it's all about them, we think they love themselves.

The truth is that their magnification of the big "I" is an attempt to pamper, pet, and pity a hungry soul that needs these things in order to compensate for the sense of incompleteness and incapability. They just don't know that they are somebody, that they are complete in Him.

If we are complete, we don't have to fight for the big end of the stick. We are already blessed, so we give the best to others. We don't try to prove our preeminence, because we already have our throne under the King of kings, so we prefer and promote others instead of ourselves.

We don't seek greatness, because we already have it. Greater is He that is in us, than he that is in the world!

"From whence come wars and fightings among you? Come they not hence, even of your lusts that war in your members? Ye lust and have not. Ye...desire to have and cannot obtain. Ye fight and war, yet ye have not..."

James 4:1-2

Disrespect, Drama, and Demands

The above verse makes it very clear to me that all human conflict comes from this lust, or void that we are talking about. It is the cause of every drama, from national military wars, to church splits, to family squabbles.

Everybody *needs* something, *demands* something, or *wants* something that they are just not getting. *Lust!*

Remember, you are not delivered from lust just because you will to stop lusting. You are not delivered from lust just because you are told to stop lusting. You are not delivered because you know it's wrong to lust.

The only deliverance from lust is fullness! You can fight lust with all of your might, but if you are not full, you will still want. We were not created to settle for an empty hole in our soul.

We were all created with this sense of inner greatness. We all feel that we are better than what we've been showing to the world. It's the secret hidden from the ages. It's Christ in you. It's the light of God's glory within you.

We all have it, but it often doesn't show on the outside, so we try to project it and prove it to others.

I can recall many times in my life when I did things that were so foolish that they were clownish. At times I was mocked and made fun of. I felt misunderstood. I wasn't that dumb. You've got me all wrong. I'm not really like that. Sometimes the drama could escalate into physical confrontation.

But despite all of my protest, the proof said I *was* that way. I was a sad contradiction over and over. I dropped out of high school, but swore that I was extremely smart. I quit job after job, but swore that I wasn't lazy. I was jailed for crimes, but swore that I was a good man. I had no skills or accomplishments, but swore that I was gifted.

I felt like a persecuted, misunderstood hero. I was totally frustrated. The world was against me. I needed respect, acceptance, worthiness; and I wasn't getting it. I lusted after it.

This carried way over into my relationship with God after I was saved. I continued to lust after respect and acceptance from God, things I already had, but didn't feel, except in short temporary spasms.

Even in ministry I lusted after it. I lusted after validation by other "known" ministers. I wanted recognition, and couldn't seem to get it. I wanted more success and a bigger congregation as God's proof that I was anointed. I was always inflating the attendance numbers in my church. When there were 50, I called it 70. Then, when I actually had 70, it was still not enough so it became 100. When we grew to 100, it was still too small, so I told my friends 150. 200 became 300.

The frustration of my lust would sometimes cause me to launch attacks from the pulpit on other ministries. It was my way of elevating me above them.

It's interesting to note that I never attacked or criticized a church smaller than mine, only those that looked more successful.

The truth is, I was already experiencing a degree of the recognition and success that I wanted so badly, but it was never enough. My lust made my attaining seem like lack. More would not satisfy. Only the real revelation of Jesus Christ would do that.

When you know that you are somebody in Christ Jesus, you don't have to become somebody. When you know you are complete in Him, you are full!

I used to feel pressure to make people believe in me. I thought then they would follow. I tried hard to project strength and perfection, but my weaknesses were always exposed.

Now, it doesn't matter to me if people believe in me. I believe in them, and I am free to love them and bless them without any personal demands or expectations from them. I have no drama with anybody.

I feel loved all of the time. I don't have to become what I already am. Yet, knowing this has caused my outer life to become more and more like my inner man.

I feel very successful now, even though I continue toward more that the Lord has for me. I am not driven by anything ugly. I am blessed to be a blessing. It doesn't have to be about me anymore. Now my life can be more about you.

Fullness!

Chapter 7

The Way of Cain

"Woe unto them for they have gone the way of Cain..."

Jude 1:11.

After the fall of man, Eve had a son and named him Cain, announcing, "I have gotten a man from the Lord."

The word *"gotten"* means *purchased, attained, or bought*. Cain's name comes from the same word.

The woman thought that she had procured this child in some way, apparently thinking she had earned this blessing.

The same woman, who thought she could attain the likeness of God, still had a performance mentality. Even after seeing the results of her ignorance, she continued to strive for the blessing and favor of God, something that cannot be earned, but is freely given.

I don't know what it was, but she obviously had been working hard to get back into God's favor. To the eastern cultures of the bible, a child was a sure sign of such favor.

Think through her mind for a moment. She knows she has displeased the Lord. She knows she has caused a lot of trouble. She wants to make it right, so she does things to please and appease God. Whatever her good works were, they were things that she assumed He wanted.

It could have been anything. In today's church it might be lots of prayer, fasting, giving, doing good, denying pleasures, worship, witnessing; anything that promises to procure favor from God.

When the child is born, Eve is sure that this blessing is because of her good deeds.

But then she has another son, Abel, which means *"empty, or nothing"*. Notice the contrast. While she purchased the first child, she did nothing to earn the second child. I believe she came to a place in life where either she stopped trying to get blessed, or she knew she just had not been living that great, but she got blessed anyway. This child came not from her goodness, but from the goodness of God. This was a child of grace.

Cain was a dirt farmer. He worked hard. By the dusty sweat of his brow he dug and tilled the earth. His soil stained hands were calloused. His sun baked back was sore. His knees were worn raw.

Abel tended sheep. On a typical day he would take a walk and the sheep would follow. He would find a place by the water to sit under the shade of a tree, and the sheep would eat and drink. He was probably home in time for a delightful supper featuring some of those delicious Cain-raised veggies.

Call me lazy, but given the choice, I would take Abel's job over Cain's.

There came a time when they both gave an offering to worship the Lord. The Bible says that God respected Abel's worship, but not Cain's. Cain became so depressed, frustrated, and jealous that he killed his brother. Why?

Cain was a good man!

I'm going to say something now that I've never heard anyone else say, ever. I submit to you that Cain was a good man. Cain was just like most of us who love the Lord, who serve Him with passion, who pray every day, and attend church every time the doors are open.

Remember, Cain was giving an offering to the Lord, not some false god. Cain was a worshiper of the one true God.

Notice also that Cain freely gave of the fruit of his labors. There was no law. He could have kept it all for himself, but he wanted to please God.

Cain had worked hard for his offering. He had spent his strength and his sweat, and now he had something good to offer to the Lord. Surely, God would be pleased. The One who knows all, knows how hard it was to get to this point. Surely, God would now reward Cain for his diligence, sacrifice, and self denial. Cain has passed his tests. His patience has been tried, but he has prevailed unto harvest. The labor was hard, but God will respect that. He will be pleased, and it will have all been worth it.

This is the day that Cain has been looking forward to. Today he will receive his blessing. Those around will witness God's favor upon Cain, for nobody has put more into their worship than this faithful firstborn son.

Cain looks over at his poor brother who is offering sheep. Abel's offering has cost him virtually nothing. No work, no sweat, no sacrifice. Will God be angry with such worthless worship? Cain's only real concern on this day is that the Lord would not be too hard on his lazy little brother.

Meanwhile, at the other altar, Abel is thinking "Lord, I have done *nothing* to deserve anything from you. If you show me favor today, it is all because of your goodness, and not my own. It's not about me. It's all about you".

"By faith Abel offered unto God a more excellent sacrifice than Cain..."

Hebrews 11:4

"...And the Lord had respect unto Abel and to his offering, but unto Cain and to his offering He had not respect"

Genesis 4:4-5

Obviously, Cain is totally surprised at God's response to the two forms of worship offered. He doesn't understand. It makes no sense. He gave the best that he could. If that's not good enough, then what is?

Cain was exhausted. He did all he knew to do. It's too hard to get to that place of God's favor. Frustrated and hopeless, he sunk to the depths of depression and self pity. Disappointed and hurt, Cain would do what all wounded souls do. He would hurt someone else.

Fullness!

"...And wherefore slew he him? Because his own works were evil, and his brother's righteous."

I John 3:12

So Cain killed his brother, and became a fugitive and vagabond (*Hebrew:* one who wavers and wanders), dwelling in the land of Nod (wandering), which is on the east (or front) of Eden.

The east of Eden is where the entrance is. Cain spent the rest of his life near the entrance. He was as close as you can get. He was almost there. He was so close, yet never quite able to make Eden (*Hebrew:* pleasure or delight) his home.

Cain was like so many believers who are almost blessed, almost healed, almost joyful. Their house is almost saved. Prosperity is near. They can sense their ship coming in, but they've been so close for years, never quite getting there. It's like they're following a carrot on a stick.

"...they have gone in the way of Cain...clouds they are without water...without fruit...wandering stars..."

Jude 1:11-13

The way of Cain is like a cloud that promises rain, but never produces. It is a religious road that constantly beckons us to continue. Though we never see the end of the road, it assures us that we are near.

~ 56 ~

The way of Cain does not enjoy God's fullness. It tries to get it. The way of Cain does not experience Heaven on Earth. The way of Cain is needy, hungry, and passionate (lustful). His name is synonymous with "get it".

Abel lived like he already had it.

"There is a way that seemeth right unto a man, but the end thereof are the ways of death."

Proverbs 16:25

When we hear the above verse, we think of those who are walking a path of sinful revelry, sensuality, addiction, hatefulness, or crime; but those are ways that are wrong and they *seem* wrong. Even those doing such things will usually admit it is wrong.

The verse is talking about a path that seems *right*. I walked a path that seemed right. Everyone told me it was right. I swore it was right. It had to be right. Every sincere believer was going this way. It was the road pointed out by most preachers I have heard. It was the only way. I saw no other.

It was the yellow brick road. Surely the munchkins weren't wrong…

"…narrow is the way which leadeth unto life, and few there be that find it."

Matthew 7:14

Fullness!

Chapter 8

Goodbye Yellow Brick Road

"But Oz never did give nothing to the Tin Man, that he didn't, didn't already have."

Dewey Bunnell, America, 1974

The story of the Wizard of Oz illustrates a magnificent truth that the church could learn from. The message is that each character was searching (and lusting) for something they already had. They walked in ignorance of the truth that would make them free! Let's look at some parallels.

Dorothy wants to go home, so she is told by the munchkins that she must seek the wizard, who is very good and powerful, but very mysterious. The munchkins had never seen this one who rules over Oz, but they just knew that if Dorothy could make it to see him face to face, he would fulfill her desire.

As we begin our Christian life, we are often sent on a quest. We are told to seek the Lord, to seek His face. If we can just get to the place where we can have this mystical, hard to attain, super spiritual encounter with God, we will be totally fulfilled. We usually spend years knowing that we are not there yet, so we continue on, believing we are getting closer to "home".

Dorothy was told that the yellow brick road is the way to the Emerald City, where the wizard dwells. She embarks on this path loaded with trees that don't want to give up their fruit, a dark wilderness where she and her friends are demonized by flying monkeys, and an enemy that desperately wants to rid her of her shoes.

Dorothy didn't understand why the witch wanted those shoes. Like the witch said, she didn't know how to use their power anyway.

When Dorothy and her friends finally get to the city, they find that it's hard to enter into. Through many tears they gain access, and finally have their encounter with the great and powerful. It is spectacular! There is thunder, fire, smoke, and the voice of words that is as intimidating as one would expect from a ruler so powerful.

Yet, instead of a sense of joy and fullness, the travelers are made to feel inadequate. They still haven't done enough! The wizard gives them still another test to prove their worthiness. They had already passed several tests, but it's never enough!

When will your testing be enough? Have you reached the end of your trials, or is there just one more ahead of you. Maybe you are stuck in a cycle that promises fullness, but has no finish line.

So Dorothy and her friends go and pass another test. Still they are denied.

Then the little dog pulls back the veil, and they all see that they have been pursuing an illusion that has no real power.

They have no other options. Disappointed, they realize that they will never reach the place of fulfillment.

Then it happens. They are shown that what they hungered for, they already had, and if they had known that in the beginning, they would never have had to make the journey.

When Dorothy finds out that she has possessed the power to go "home" all along, she asks Glinda (the good witch), "Why didn't you tell me?"

To which Glinda replied, "You had to find out for yourself".

Fullness!

That's why we all take that road through the wilderness. We have to come to our own revelation of what we possess in Christ Jesus the Lord. The road really takes you to the end of you. What you find at the end of the road, is a real understanding that what you needed, you had all the time!

"You have not come to a place like Mount Sinai...There is no flaming fire or dark cloud or storm...The sight was so frightening that Moses said he shook with fear. You have now come to Mount Zion and to the heavenly Jerusalem. This is the city of the living God..."

Hebrews 12:18-22 CEV

Chapter 9

Key to the Kingdom: Only the Rich Get Richer

"For he that hath, to him shall be given; and he that hath not, from him shall be taken away even that which he hath"

Mark 4:25

The verse above is one that I skipped over for years. It just didn't make sense. It sounded like the rich just get richer, while the poor keep losing. It seemed to violate the purpose of the kingdom of God. It seemed to go against the very heart of God.

It looks like the Robin Hood system of the Bizarro world, robbing from the poor and giving to the rich.

But this verse was no aberration. We see it again as Jesus tells the parable of the talents. Again, He says to take from the poor and give to the rich.

Then how can those who are needy ever rise up? If you must *have* in order to increase, what about those with nothing?

Your perception determines your reality!

Pay very close attention to what may be the most powerful key to the kingdom of Heaven! Those who use the keys don't need to break through.

Those who *have* are those who *believe* they have. They have a *perception* of abundance. It's a matter of faith. They know that God has given them all things that pertain to life and godliness (II Pet. 1:3).

Those who have not, are those who believe they are needy. They have a perception of lack, and as long as they desire to have (lust), they cannot receive, because lust will never fill their need.

"...thy faith may become effectual by the acknowledging of every good thing that is in you in Christ Jesus"

Philemon 6

Jesus once wanted to feed thousands of people. His disciples begged to send them home. There was no way to feed them. It would be an impossible situation. They explained to Jesus that **they did not have enough** to feed them.

The Lord, who is the author of abundant life, who gives us the keys to this kingdom, simply went to work on the heavenly principle of increase.

Instead of focusing on their lack, Jesus made the disciples tell Him what they *did* have, which was only a few loaves of bread and fish. He then gave thanks to the God who is more than enough, the One who can do more than we can ask or think.

Jesus was thankful that He had something. He was thanking the Father that there was more than enough to feed the multitude, because if you have *something* you're about to get more!

When carnal-brained disciples look at five loaves of bread, they see "not enough". When sons look at it, they see more than enough for they are abundance minded, not need and desire minded.

"A little one shall become a thousand"

Isaiah 60:22

When God created us and put us in the Garden of Eden, He blessed us and commanded us to be fruitful, multiply, have dominion and subdue the earth. We are created for increase, so that God's will can be done on earth as it is in Heaven!

My friends, this principle of increase works automatically. It is Christ-likeness. It is how this kingdom operates and multiplies. It is the key that so many overlook as they try other things.

I visited a man in the hospital once. One of the sweetest, loving, pious men I've met. He couldn't understand why the physical affliction was happening to him. He had suffered for years and now it was worse than ever. He didn't know why someone who loved God so much had to suffer as he did.

I tried to explain that it's not a matter of affection, sacrifice or even pure motives. It is a matter of faith. Our mind has to be renewed so that it thinks like Jesus. Only the truth will make us free!

Second Kings, chapter four, tells us the story of a woman whose husband had died, leaving her in debt and unable to pay her bills. She pleaded with the prophet Elisha to help her, citing how her husband feared the Lord.

She looked to Elisha for help, because God seemed to hear his prayers more than hers. He had the magic touch. He was God's anointed. If God would do it for anyone, it would be him. It was her only chance.

But I love what Elisha did. Instead of waving his magic wand, and fixing her situation for her, he took the opportunity to set her up for life, to teach her how it's done. He gave her the keys!

"So Elisha said to her, 'What shall I do for you? Tell me, what do you have in the house?' And she said, 'Your maidservant has nothing in the house but a jar of oil.'"

II Kings 4:2 NKJV

After the woman told him what she needed, what she did not have, he redirected her thinking. He got her to focus on what she *did* have.

Why? Because to him who has, more shall be given, but to him that has not, even what he has will be lost.

That's why the more this woman prayed, the worse her situation became. It also explains why so many people who love God continue to suffer lack and need.

The woman said she had *nothing* but a jar of oil. What she thought was insufficient, was actually more than enough! Her problem was that she was operating from lack rather than abundance.

Elisha did what any preacher worth his salt should do. He taught her that all she needed, she already had. He taught her how to make a little become a lot.

When you understand that God gives everything in the form a seed, you can begin to understand that all you need, you already have.

When Jesus' disciples asked for great faith, He gave them a mustard seed.

He said the kingdom of Heaven was like a seed, a miracle multiplying machine.

I know a lot of people are praying that God will make them a millionaire, waiting for Him to transfer wealth into their hands. What they don't know, is that He has already put the millions into their hands, in the form a seed!

Because it looks like so little to them, they just spend it on wants and needs instead of using it to make more, and they usually go deeper into debt. They need to know that the little bit is a blessing, and it can make them rich if they have the vision of income and *increase* instead of income and *outgo*.

The only difference between the poor and the rich is what they do with their little bit.

"The blessing of the Lord, it maketh rich, and He addeth no sorrow with it"

Proverbs 10:22

The Lord used a personal lesson to make this truth concrete in my mind. I used to have fits of frustration over traffic lights. I was convinced that I was cursed. I seemed to catch every red light, especially if I was in a hurry. I would even declare how they "saw me coming" when they would turn red right before I got there. I spoke like they did it on purpose.

Then, during one of my rants, bemoaning my luck, I heard the Lord say *"You curse every red light you get, but you've never once been thankful or even acknowledged a green light"*.

My heart broke. I knew I was being a baby, and I should have known better than to curse my situation. I also realized that I was indirectly blaming God, because I felt like He could do something about it if He wanted to, but He never did.

I saw that I was only compounding my lack of green lights by focusing on the red. I immediately repented, vowing to change my thinking and my speech.

I couldn't wait for my next green light. I would celebrate it, thereby creating more green lights. When I finally came to a green light, cruising right through it, I joyfully thanked the Lord aloud.

My wife looked at me like aliens had taken over my body.

Soon my luck was changing. It was so obviously different! Even friends who have ridden with me have noted it.

Fullness!

I have found the key, and my life has not been the same since!

Another example

There was a couple in a church where I have preached often. They were invited to minister at another church hundreds of miles away, in another state.

As they talked it over between them, they thought they would have to decline the invitation. Their vehicle was an old, undependable van that didn't even have reverse.

But they remembered the Word of the Lord, and decided that, instead of staying home for a lack of transportation, they would celebrate what they *did* have.

What they did have was a van that started when they turned the key, and it went forward when they put it in gear. It wasn't much, but it was *something*, and they decided that it was more than enough.

Forgetting what they needed, and acknowledging what they *did* have, they went ahead and did the meeting. The next day, someone in that church gave them a new SUV, which they drove home. A little bit became a lot!

Had they continued to focus on their lack, rather than celebrate what they did have, they would still be driving the old van today, if it still runs.

Just think of all of the blessings that humanity does without because we are a fallen race with a fallen mindset.

But thanks be to God who gives us new life, makes us a new man, and renews our mind!

Let's change the way we pray.

Most of our prayers are acknowledgments of need. Need-based prayers only perpetuate lack. That's why Christians go from one problem to the next.

If you are sick, acknowledge the health that you *do* have. He that has gets more.

If you are poor, be thankful for what you *do* have, because a little becomes a lot in the kingdom of abundant living.

These are the thoughts of a mind renewed. We are not cursed. We are blessed. The good is increasing, and our future is bright!

Once you become whole on the inside, the outside has to follow. This kingdom manifests from the inside out.

You are complete in Him. All you need is in your "house". You don't have to go searching for it.

Fullness!

You just need to know what you already have through Jesus Christ.

"...His divine power hath given unto us all things that pertain unto life and godliness..."

I Peter 1:3

Chapter 10

The Third Day

"Be not ignorant of this one thing, that one day is with the Lord as a thousand years, and a thousand years as one day. The Lord is not slack concerning His promise..."

II Peter 3:8-9

The calendar has changed! Very recently, sometime in this decade, after the year 2000, we entered the third thousand year period since Christ. It marked the beginning of the era of fullness!

It's here! According to the calculator in the above verse you can count on it. God is not slack concerning this promise, as some men count slackness. It is the third day from Christ, seventh day from Adam. It's the day of completion, fullness and rest. It's the third and final dimension for sons of God to come into.

There is no greater day! It's better than revival, better than any move of God, Old or New Testament. It goes beyond the gifts of the Spirit, and into abundant life, heavenly living!

"After two days He will revive us, in the third day He will raise us up, and we shall live in His sight."

Hosea 6:1-2

The Three Spiritual Dimensions

- The Way – The Truth – The Life
- Death – Burial – Resurrection
- Body – Soul – Spirit
- Outer Court – Inner Court – Holy of Holies
- Doubt – Hope - Faith
- Egypt – Wilderness – Promised Land

These all speak of a progression from the least to the greatest. They all speak the same message, and each part goes along with its counterpart in the other examples. For instance: *The Life, Resurrection, Spirit, Holy of Holies, Faith, and Promised Land* all speak of the same thing. They all speak of that third day, or third dimension, or third level of your destiny.

Let's use *Egypt – Wilderness – Promised Land* to illustrate.

Egypt represents doubt, the lowest level you can be on. There is nothing good there.

The wilderness represents hope. You have left the land of doubt, and you are going somewhere. Life is still hard, but you know that you have been promised something better, so you journey on. You don't live in abundance, but God does enough miracles to keep you going. You have accumulated a lot of testimonies here, but the best is yet to come.

Hope is great, but the wilderness is not home. Home is the land that has been promised to you. Hope has power. It keeps you from quitting when you're tired. It gets you through a lot of trials, but it's always looking to the future. It's always "someday", "over yonder", "in the sweet bye and bye". God is "just about to do something". Better things are "just around the corner". You feel like God is going to heal you "any day now". Your financial ship is about to come in. You're following a carrot on a stick. You're almost there, almost healed, almost blessed. You're almost prosperous.

The third level is the Promised Land, the holy of holies, the third heaven. It's the most perfect place. It's the seventh day rest. It's the place of completion and the finished work. It's the land of unadulterated faith.

Fullness!

This faith is not to be confused with the hope of the wilderness. This faith does not say "tomorrow", but "now". In this place the kingdom of Heaven is at hand!

If you are alive today you are living in this third day. You now have to embrace it and adopt its way of operation. There are many people living in this land of milk and honey, but don't know it, so they are scratching around for manna. To operate in this day you have to have a new day mindset. That's why God told Moses to *"Let them be ready for the third day"* (Exodus 19:11).

All things are ready and the calendar has changed, but you can't bring wilderness belief systems into this day. You have to drop them off into the Jordan River and have a new expectation.

This is **"the now zone".**

"...what is this proverb that you people have...which says, the days are prolonged and every vision fails? Tell them therefore, Thus says the Lord God, I will lay this proverb to rest, and they shall no more use it... But say to them, the days are at hand, and the fulfillment of every vision... and the word which I speak will come to pass, it will no more be postponed"

Ezekiel 12:22-25

Chapter 11

The Now Zone

"Behold, the days come, saith the Lord, that the plowman shall overtake the reaper, and the treader of grapes him that soweth seed..."

Amos 9:13

That mouthful of scripture simply tells us that the time would come when things would happen so fast that there would be no waiting between sowing and reaping. As soon as the seed hits the ground, the harvest is hitting you in the face!

Another key to this wonderful, glorious, abundant kingdom is the power of *now*. It is the falling away of the mindset that puts everything off into the future, thereby forfeiting the possibility of instant change.

In the former season we learned to be patient. We all needed to learn it. There is no heavenly peace without it, and being anxious about something never produces anything.

However, we also became accustomed to waiting. It became a normal part of our existence. God wants to put an end to waiting.

Now vs. Later – Faith vs. Hope

Faith always speaks in the present. Hope is always later. Hope says we will have it…later.

Hope is good. Don't get me wrong. It keeps you going when you want to quit. It keeps looking at a prize down the road. It gets you through the hard times, but hope is not home. We are not supposed to live there. Our inheritance is in the land of milk and honey, the third dimension of the spirit. I call it "the now zone".

God's name, Jehovah, means to *exist* or *be*. He calls Himself "I Am". He first reveals this to Moses when He is about to deliver Israel out of Egypt.

"…when I come unto the children of Israel, and shall say unto them, 'The God of our fathers has sent me unto you', and they shall say unto me, 'What is His name?' What shall I say unto them?

And God said unto Moses, "I AM THAT I AM, and He said, 'Thus shall you say unto the children of Israel, I AM has sent me unto you'."

Exodus 3:13-14

Also, in Exodus chapter 6 the Lord says the patriarchs knew Him as God Almighty, but not by His name, Jehovah (I Am).

This is very important. In order to bring about a long awaited deliverance, God had to reveal Himself as the God of now, not later. The Israelites knew deliverance was coming someday. They just did not know it was *this* day.

In the same way, we have to turn the corner in our thinking. God is the God of *now*, not later, or down the road, or over yonder, or in the sweet by and by, or in another dispensation. He's not even the God of the next awesome move of God. His name is *Now*!

In Luke chapter 4 Jesus was asked to read from scripture in the synagogue one Sabbath day. He read from Isaiah about the promise of the coming of the Christ. I'm sure their hope was stirred with longing for such a deliverance to come. Broken hearts would be healed. Blind eyes would be opened. What a day that would be!

But when Jesus announced that the time was now, confusion and even anger filled the air. The carnal mind doesn't want to make the transition into the day of fullness. It simply has to die.

Wherever Jesus went, He brought the people's waiting to an end. He was only doing what He saw the Father do.

"For all the promises of God in Him are yea, and in Him amen..."

II Corinthians 1:20

Time Shall Be No More!

You will find that this revelation of fullness has power to bring about every promise of God now, without waiting!

Up until now, time has been a buffer between you and answers to prayer. You prayed then you waited (time), then sometime later you may have gotten what you prayed for.

The pattern has always been: *seed*, then *time* (waiting), then *harvest*; but God is now taking *time* out of the equation! He said He would do this. The reaping and sowing would come together. When you receive the revelation of fullness, your equation becomes: *seed-harvest* (no *time* in between).

"And it shall come to pass, that before they call, I will answer, and while they are yet speaking, I will hear."

Isaiah 65:24

High Definition, High Speed Spirituality

Though I point out some shortcomings of our present spirituality, I'm not necessarily calling it wrong. It's just that there is better.

John the Baptist had a ministry that was not wrong. It was necessary, and the right thing for the time, but it was not the best. There was something better, quicker, more powerful and efficient.

"Among those that are born of women, there is not a greater prophet than John the Baptist, but he that is least in the kingdom of God is greater than he."

Luke 7:28

The IBM Selectric was a wonderful typewriter. It was the cutting edge machine of its day, but if you are using one today, you are robbing yourself of efficiency and quality. Now you can use a quicker computer keyboard, click send, and send thousands of documents around the world in the same time and with less effort than before.

God has changed the technology in the spirit as well. I have won many battles through spiritual warfare. I believe it saved my life at times, but I needed to do warfare because I was living on the same plane as my spiritual enemies. Now I rarely even hear the voice of my adversary the devil.

*"And a **high**way shall be there...No lion shall be there, nor any ravenous beast shall go up thereon, it shall not be found there; but the redeemed shall walk there."*

Isaiah 35:8-9

I love this *high*er way!

I've seen many prayers answered through groaning and travail in the Spirit. Now I see better and quicker results through thanksgiving. I love this life!

God has prepared us to be a "now" people. We like fast food, one hour cleaners, and high speed internet. We are called to something fresh and better.

We Are Different

This is the day of fullness. I know that some of the things I say are different, but I am different. I see differently so I operate differently.

I believe we are different as a generation. We are breaking a pattern that has been set for quite a while. We are not repeating the patterns of hunger and longing. We are setting a new paradigm.

The Now Zone

We are *the reaping generation...*

Fullness!

Chapter 12

The Reaping Generation

"Say not ye, There are yet four months, and then cometh harvest? Behold, I say unto you, Lift up your eyes, and look on the fields, for they are white already to harvest."

John 4:35

This move is the last move! It's here! We are not in preparation for something more awesome down the road. This is the season whereby the sons of God can stand and minister from a position of fullness and completion.

We have become so accustomed to the journey, that it really seemed that the attainment of the apex would never be realized. We thought everybody just eventually dies somewhere along the upward climb, never experiencing the fullness anytime in this life.

But creation has been groaning for us to come into our own, and it won't groan much longer. We are coming! The sons of God are being unveiled.

God is revealing knowledge to us. It is knowledge of who we are, what we have, and knowledge to discern this time and season.

I know one thing. It is not time to continue to redo what has already been done. New things are springing forth with new knowledge and a fresh anointing. We have the *finishing* anointing.

*"My meat is to do the will of Him that sent Me, and to **finish** His work."*

John 4:34

Jesus shows us how to finish. He knew what his portion was. He didn't try to copy any Old Testament ministry. He didn't try to bring back a move of the Spirit as in the old days. He didn't try to be like the hot ministry of the day, John the Baptist.

He came to reap what was sown and prepared by the Father. Wherever Jesus went He brought a heavenly manifestation of healing, freedom, joy, etc. He demonstrated that the kingdom of Heaven was at hand (now).

Jesus came along and partook of the fruit (manifestation) of a tree that He didn't have to plant or grow. The Father had already seen to that, and since Jesus knew that all things were prepared, all He had to do was finish.

I think we, the church, have been praying a lot of prayers that have already been prayed. We are replicating spiritual labor that has already been labored. We are trying to break a barrier that One has already broken. We are seeking outpourings that have already fallen. We are aspiring to ministries that we've already heard.

Let's break the pattern and be something new!

"I sent you to reap that whereupon you bestowed no labor"

John 4:38

How is that for a new pattern? Can you dig it?

Well, I'm telling you that you have the reaping anointing. You attract people, blessing, and favor. Joy, health, and all that is in the Father's house attach themselves to your person. You partake of it and you dispense it. Freely you receive, and freely you can give it.

More Than We've Labored For

In Matthew, chapter 20, Jesus said that the kingdom of Heaven was like a man who went out to hire laborers for his vineyard. He hired some at six in the morning for a day's pay. Then at nine, twelve, and three o'clock he hired others, telling them that he would give them "what is right".

Finally, at five o'clock, he did the same with others he had found.

At the end of the day all were paid, and to everybody's surprise, those who came at the eleventh hour (five o'clock) received a full day's pay.

It wasn't fair. Those who had to labor through the high sun at midday complained that these eleventh hour people came at the time of the evening breeze (Genesis calls it "the cool of the day").

"They shall hunger no more, neither thirst any more, neither shall the sun light on them, nor any heat."
Revelation 7:16

The owner said that he could choose to be good to them if he wants to. It might not be "fair". It certainly wasn't less than fair. It was more than fair! You can be sure that those last-hour people enjoyed it.

God wants to be good to you. He wants you to have more than you labored for, prayed for, and put in time for. He wants you to reap where you have not sown.

I know that the principle of sowing and reaping will always work, but wow, this is a whole new level! It's a new rule for a new day!

We Get Paid For All Former Generations!

When God sent Moses to deliver Israel out of Egypt, they had been there for over 400 years.

God had promised Abraham that his descendants would have the land of Canaan, but these descendants never set one foot on it. Generation after generation held to the promise, passing it down to the next, who also would not see it come to pass.

Then the day came when God brought them out with all of the silver and gold of Egypt, and He healed them all. There was not one feeble among their tribes.

I believe that God did not have to steal from Egypt in order to give all of the gold to the Israelites. He is not a thief, and He is just. His scales are perfectly balanced.

I believe that God calculated 430 years of unpaid wages, and made payment in one day. The reaping generation gets everything! The full day's pay!

For all of the saints who died not receiving the promise, somebody has to get paid. For those who believed God would heal them yet they died, someone has to get paid. For all of those who went before us, who labored, who fought the good fight, who denied themselves, and who kept the faith even when it looked like God was a liar, somebody has to get paid.

Fullness!

This is how God will be glorified. This world will look upon you as a showcase of His goodness!

This generation gets it all. Fullness!

"And these all, having obtained a good report through faith, received not the promise; God having provided some better thing for us, that they without us should not be made perfect"

Hebrews 11:39-30

What they worked for is not completed unless we get paid for their labors.

I have no qualms about receiving the good things of God that I don't deserve. I understand that my calling and my anointing is to receive fullness. I did not earn what I have. It is my inheritance.

"Fear not little flock, for it is your father's good pleasure to give you the kingdom."

Luke 12:32

God has promised to fill this "latter house" with greater glory than the former. He didn't say that the house would be greater. In fact, in Haggai chapter 2, He said this house was *not* greater. Yet, the glory would be greater!

In Deuteronomy chapter 6, The Lord said He would give us cities we did not build, wells that we didn't dig, and trees that we didn't plant. We are the reaping generation!

"When we don't get what we deserve
That's a real good thing, a real good thing
When we get what we don't deserve
That's a real good thing, a real good thing"
"Real Good Thing" Newsboys 1994

Fullness!

Chapter 13

The Heaven-Earth Realm

"...it is time to seek the Lord, till He come and rain righteousness upon you."

Hosea 10:12

When God made Heaven and Earth, the sky was a firmament, or *expanse* that divided the waters above from the waters beneath (Gen. 1:7). It did not rain in those days. The ground was watered by a mist that came up from the earth.

The division between the water above and the water beneath symbolizes the separation between God and man, His Spirit and our soul. His ways were higher than our ways. His thoughts were higher than our thoughts. Man has tried to breach that firmament through various religions, each one founded on the knowledge of good and evil, resulting in striving.

Fullness!

"And the Lord said, My spirit shall not always strive with man..."

Genesis 6:3

Later, when Noah entered the ark, God opened the heavens. The waters above became one with the waters below. Together they created a flood.

Science teaches us that any rain that falls to the earth was already on the earth. It evaporates and rises, creating clouds, then falls again. It is a never ending cycle.

After God opened the heavens, He never had to open it again. The earth now has all it needs to produce rain.

When God poured out His Spirit on the day of Pentecost, He never had to pour it out again. It is available to whosoever will, and it is here!

All that we need, we already have.

Never again do we have to pray the heavens open. Jesus split the veil between our world and God's world! He has pierced the heavens, and we now live under an open heaven!

Two worlds become one!

Once the waters above mingled with the waters below, the two became one.

"But he that is joined unto the Lord is one spirit"
I Corinthians 6:17.

When Jesus split the veil a wonderful thing happened. God remodeled His temple (you). He made two small rooms into one big room.

The glory that was once confined beyond the veil flooded the sanctuary (our soul). God's world became a part of your world, and your world became a part of heaven. There are no longer two rooms inside the tabernacle, but one.

I used to teach on the tabernacle of Moses with my charts and transparencies. The floor plan had that veil in the way, separating God's world from the one we operate in. I would point to the lesser side of that veil and declare that our position was on the weak side. So God wants us to break through to the other side via worship, or prayer, or holiness, or self denial.

On occasions, we would have a holy of holies experience, a glimpse of glory. We would "spy out the land" so to speak, but never stay there.

I've got good news! You don't have to journey into the most holy place. It came to you! What you could not do, Jesus did for you! Heaven has come to your world. Enjoy it!

The key to the kingdom is revelation knowledge. Revelation means *unveiled*. All you need is the knowledge of the unveiling of God's glory. He didn't want you to make a journey into His world. He wanted to bring His world to yours, and He did!

Do you see how our mindset has to change? The hungry church is trying to get into that place. They don't have a revelation of what they already have. If they knew, they would wake up every day rejoicing in the light of God's glory!

"Then the glory of the Lord went up from the cherub, and stood over the threshold of the house; and the house was filled with the cloud, and the court was filled with the brightness of the Lord's glory"

Ezekiel 10:4.

New Heaven and New Earth

The removal of the barrier between God's world and ours has created the new Heaven and new Earth that John saw when the Lord opened his eyes to the revelation of Jesus Christ.

God showed this to me in a night vision once. I found myself in Heaven, feeling all of the joy that you would expect. I didn't know how I got there. I didn't know if I had died or had just been caught up. It didn't matter, and I didn't give it any thought.

Heaven was like a park. There were picnic tables and a body of water with sailboats.

A word about heavenly visions: Heaven is too grandiose for anyone to confine it to a physical description. When we have a vision like this, it seems that we all experience it symbolically in a way that speaks to us individually. I never take someone's physical description literally.

After a while, I found myself walking and talking with Jesus, just enjoying fellowship. We sat down at a table which had a stack of blocks at one end.

He told me to knock them off of the table. When I did, the blocks fell to the ground landing on top of each other in a perfect stack.

Jesus said, "That's how it is in the kingdom of Heaven".

We continued to talk and sometime later, I accidentally bumped the stack with my arm. They fell to the ground in a sloppy pile.

I said, "How could that happen here?"

To which He replied, "You just forgot where you were, try it again."

Of course, when I did it again they fell into perfect order.

Over the course of this experience which seemed to last for days though it never was night, I repeatedly asked the Lord if I was dreaming.

He assured me with the same answer each time, "This is not a dream. This is real, and this will never end."

But eventually, I *did* wake up. I sat up in my bed, disappointed. I was so sure it was real this time. It was too good. It was painful to wake up back in Earth life.

I said, "Lord it seemed too real. It's so depressing to know that I was only dreaming."

Then I heard His Spirit speak resoundingly in my ear saying, "This is not a dream. This is real, and this will never end."

Since then, it has not been so difficult to remember where I am. The kingdom is among us. This is real, and my life has never been the same.

> *"Earth's crammed with heaven,*
> *And every common bush afire with God;*
> *But only he who sees, takes off his shoes..."*
> Elizabeth Barrett Browning

Chapter 14

The Day of the Lord

"We have also a more sure word of prophecy, whereunto ye do well that ye take heed, as unto a light that shineth in a dark place, until the day dawn, and the daystar arise in your hearts."

II Peter 1:19

This is it! The last revival! The move you have been praying for. There has not been a day like this, nor will there ever be. You made it. It's here. We will not need another one after this. It will culminate with us seeing the Lord face to face in all of His glory!

I have prophesied for decades that this day would come. I spoke of "the glory of the latter house". I decreed that this was the greatest generation to ever be alive. I saw a glorious church looking like Jesus, doing His works and greater.

I can no longer prophesy that message, because that day is here! All I can do now is announce it to all who can hear.

This move is nothing like I thought it would be, but it's better than I could have imagined. It's better than anything the church has ever had before!

Like a Thief in the Night

The Lord always comes in a way that we would not think. He was born in a stable. The religious people who were looking for the Christ in that day missed Him because He did not come in the way they expected. They looked for a political military leader, not this pacifist teacher who wasn't even a good Jew as far as they were concerned.

In the same way, we have a lot of good people anticipating an awesome restoring move of God. They are hungry for the revival to beat all revivals, and they declare they will press on until they see it, not settling for anything less.

The problem is, they don't know what the move will look like. They might think they do, but they don't. They speak of and pray for outward manifestations, trying to imagine what the revival will be like, but their minds have only former moves to compare it with, so they think it will be like some great revival of the past only more intense.

This move is not in the thunder, or the lightning, or an earthquake. It is a still small voice. Many are missing this greatest move because it is not spectacular enough. It is too anticlimactic.

The last revival is the *unveiling* of Christ in you. It's the uncovering of the One who has been covered for so long. It's the glory of the Lord rising upon you from the inside out. It's the Sun of righteousness arising with healing in His wings. It's Jacob becoming Israel. It's struggling Christianity becoming the glorious church!

I thought all of my seeking, hungering, and thirsting would lead me to some super spectacular something. Instead, it brought me to a revelation, a knowing and a conviction that He loves me. My journey has ended, and this knowledge has filled my heart with joy and faith, changing the world around me into a heavenly realm.

This is the dawning of a new day! God has brought you through so much to get you to this day. You have come into the kingdom for such a time as this.

Your Secret Is Revealed

The Lord said that there is nothing secret that will not be revealed. He said anything hidden will be made manifest.

Man, how that used to scare me! There were too many things I hoped God would just keep between us.

However, I later realized that the greatest secret that's been hidden from the ages is Christ in us! It's the glory of God that has been kept secret. It's who we really are! The world thinks we are just members of a club that likes to pray, preach, and sing Jesus songs; but they are about to see that "now are we the sons of God"!

Your dreams are about to be made manifest. Fullness! Those promises God made to you, that you've kept *hidden* in your heart are about to happen! He's bringing them out of the secret place and into the outer court, where all will see it!

The day of the Lord is when the sun arises in your heart. Then it is seen upon you. It's the unveiling of something, or should I say someone, that has been covered for too long.

When The Lord Reveals Himself, He Reveals You!

This is a truth we see repeated throughout the Bible. When the Lord revealed Himself to Sarah's husband, it changed Abram to Abraham. It changed Saul of Tarsus to Paul the apostle. When it was revealed to Simon that Jesus was the Christ, Jesus in turn revealed that Simon was Peter the rock.

When the Lord shows you who He is, you see who you are!

"But we all, with open face beholding as in a glass the glory of the Lord, are changed into the same image..."

II Corinthians 5:18

It happened to Jacob at a brook called Jabbok (pouring out), when he wrestled with the LORD all night *until the day dawned.*

He wouldn't let go until God blessed him. His daddy, Isaac, had promised that the day would come when he would get the blessing, and when it happened, Jacob would no longer be a stranger in the land of inheritance.

Like Jacob, we have held to a promise of blessing. We also have an inheritance, it's the kingdom of Heaven; but like Jacob most of us are still a stranger to that place.

God blessed Jacob that night. It happened in a way that was probably different than what he thought it would be. God blessed him with a revelation. The Lord said that he would no longer be called Jacob, but Israel, which means *"one who rules as God"*.

Jacob, who thought he was about to die at the hand of his brother, was now Israel, the one destined to rule over his brother.

Fullness!

God had promised Jacob's mother that his older brother would serve him, so the ruler was always there. It was just covered up by Jacob.

You are about to enjoy your inheritance! This world is about to find out who you really are! Creation, you can stop your groaning. Look out world. We're coming!

"...There shall come a star out of Jacob, and a scepter shall rise out of Israel..."

Numbers 24:17

Chapter 15

The Sons of God: The Heaven Dwellers

"And the servant abideth not in the house forever, but the son abideth ever."

John 8:35

If you want to know how to experience the life of Christ, read the gospels. Jesus was not trying to keep the secret to Himself. He kept telling us what the Son of God does. So let's just do that.

A son does not beg. He knows that the Father loves the son, therefore whatsoever the son asks, it is done.

A son is not a servant. The kingdom of God is not a plantation that we work for. It is a family business! As heirs of God and joint heirs with Jesus

Christ, we own this kingdom. It was our Father's good pleasure to give it to us, and He is most pleased if we will receive it.

"Henceforth I call you not servants, for the servant knoweth not what his lord doeth..."

John 15:15

We are different. We know that God digs us. We are not perfect, but we have been blessed with every spiritual blessing of Heaven.

We don't need an invitation to sit at the Master's table. Our family owns the thing!

We are not concerned about being provided for. Everything in the house is ours, so our job as stewards of the family business, is to see that the things in this house are dispensed to the world around us.

A Word about Brokenness, Humility, and Death to Self

The servant mindset has to die! The incomplete mindset has to be broken! We have to humble ourselves and be willing to lay down our old ways and thoughts. This is the crucifixion of the flesh.

This is how the flesh (carnal mindset) suffers! It is put down like Jacob was put down when Israel arose. Jeremiah called it *"the time of Jacob's trouble"*.

Jacob was in trouble that night, big trouble. He didn't survive. The way that had brought him so far, only to find a dead end, was destroyed.

"Alas! For that day is great, so that none is like it. It is even the time of Jacob's trouble, but he shall be saved out of it."

Jeremiah 30:7

Suffering in the flesh doesn't have to be terrible things happening in your life. It can simply be the loss (giving up) of your life, so you can have the best life now!

True humility can look like pride to those who are stuck, but when we submit to the truth, and accept everything God says about us, we are going to live like sons and enjoy it!

It is pride to hold on to weak and beggarly living when God is offering so much more. Pride never thinks it needs to change, so it fights to stay the same.

It takes the light of God's glory shining in the darkness to break us out of its stronghold. It takes a strong Word, and that Word is busting the walls of limitation and intimidation in our belief and in our thinking.

We are being changed from the inside out. The Lord didn't say we would be changed by a revival meeting, or through fasting, or the laying on of hands. He said we would be transformed by the renewing of our minds.

Free your mind and the rest will follow. Change your mind and you will change the world!

Rescued or Empowered?

Another mindset that has to die is the rescue mentality. This is the mindset that looks "out there" for help. It focuses more on a God "out there", rather than God abiding within.

Those who have that perception are often frustrated, wondering if God hears. Does He care? When will He answer? Why doesn't He answer?

People with that mentality are usually waiting for God. To them, God is tarrying and God will do it when He's ready. While they are suffering or doing without, God is up there in His Heaven being slow.

They aren't aware that their help abides within them and all that they need, they already have. The truth is, we are not waiting on the Lord. He is waiting on us. He has planted within us the seed of the kingdom, which is Heaven on Earth, and He is now looking for the increase of the seed. He is now looking for the kingdom to manifest from the inside out.

"...the husbandman waiteth for the precious fruit of the earth..."

James 5:7

Jesus was asleep in the boat when a storm arose. His disciples, facing shipwreck, did what most of us think is a great idea. They went to have a little talk with Jesus, to tell Him about their trouble.

But they couldn't make Him move and they thought He didn't care. Most of us have had similar experiences with Him. We know He could do something about it. We're fighting and losing. So why is nothing happening? Isn't He with us? Doesn't He want us to make it to the other side? Why is this going on so long?

Jesus got up and rebuked the wind and waves, and there was peace all around.

Then Jesus turned and rebuked the disciples for not doing what He had just done.

The disciples did not do it, because they were external minded. They had a rescue mentality. They didn't know what they had. The storm around them became a storm within them, and they thought they would die. Their inner thoughts were formed by external conditions. They were conformed to the world around them.

"And be not conformed to this world: but be ye transformed by the renewing of your mind, that you may prove what is that good, and acceptable, and perfect will of God"

Romans 12:2

The Son, on the other hand, was exactly the opposite. What He had on the inside was greater than anything around Him. Instead of conforming to the storm around Him, He made the peace *within* Him become the peace *around* Him.

The world conformed to Him! Sons know how it works. The kingdom *within* you becomes the kingdom *around* you. It's not about being rescued. It's about being inwardly empowered. All that we need, we already have.

It's called FULLNESS.

Walking on Earth, Living in Heaven

We live in a totally different realm (reality) than carnal man. This realm or kingdom is the city with walls as clear as glass. It's invisible, but very real and very powerful. It's the secret place of the Most High God.

We are experiencing Heaven in ever increasing measure. It is our inheritance and we do not apologize.

You will now be a showcase for God's glory and a trophy of His goodness. Others will see, and they will be convinced the He is good!

Fullness!

Chapter 16

A Final Word on Fullness

As you embrace this new season, you will begin to notice some changes that will take some getting used to.

1. You will sense something good happening around you that is more real than any hope or expectation you've had before!
2. You will notice favor. Doors of opportunity and blessing that were hard to find will present themselves to you. (Read Isaiah 60).
3. It will be natural and easy to believe things that were so far out before. You won't feel a need to stir up your faith.
4. Your prayer life will completely change! You won't clock in to put in prayer time

as much. It will seem like you are always praying, just not in the same way as before.

5. You won't feel required to do "spiritual" things. In fact you will be so free you may almost feel guilty about not feeling guilty. You may even question your own zeal for God. Enjoy it. When we've been burdened for a long time, walking uprightly takes a little getting used to.

6. Blessings come too easy! Again, don't feel bad that you did nothing to get it. It's an average day for a son of God.

7. You will love everybody! You are so satisfied, content, and full of God that there is no reason to have any strife. Fullness is always the answer!

8. Your ears will become sensitive to any message that doesn't support your new season. That's okay. Don't be critical, but you will want to connect with those who speak your new language.

9. You will enjoy life like you never dreamed was possible!

Chapter 17

So What Do I Do Now?

To make the transition is not really that hard. Thank God that we don't have to be super strong, or super smart or super "holy". Thank God that we don't even have to attain some high, mystical, super spirituality.

"For this commandment which I command you today is not too mysterious for you, nor is it far off."
                                Deuteronomy 30:11 (NKJV)

You are simply crossing over in the spirit of your mind. You are changing the way you think and the way you view things. Your life will change from the inside out.

Here are some things you can do that will be supportive of your heavenly living:

Fullness!

1. Change how you pray. Instead of asking, try thanking God. Thanksgiving is a sign of fullness. It declares that we already have it. This is major. I have found that thankfulness is the strongest magnet for the blessings of life. A thankful person is the one who seems to have the Midas touch.

2. Acknowledge God's presence always. Don't try to "enter in". Just wake up every day and imagine an open heaven. I promise you, others will notice the heavenly atmosphere around you.

3. Take notice of the Heaven that is around you. What you focus on, increases. Acknowledging the goodness in your life not only gives you inner peace and joy, but it actually will multiply the good things around you. Start thanking God for "Heaven on Earth"!

4. Act like you have it all now! Putting it off into the future only makes you settle for less in the present.

5. Read the gospels. That's where Jesus tells us how to live like a son. Whatever He says about the Son, replace it with "the sons". We can do that because we are heirs of God and joint heirs with Christ. This is the pattern that we follow.

So What Do I Do Now?

"...See, sayeth He, that you make all things according to the pattern showed to thee..."

Hebrews 8:5

I hope that you feel that you have license to "go for it"!

I hope you feel that you have permission to live the highest and best that God has, now!

Welcome to fullness! There is no more sacrifice for sin. The labor is over. This is the rest. It's been a long time coming, but this is good...

"Surely goodness and mercy will follow me all the days of my life, and I will dwell in the house of the Lord forever."

Psalms 23:6

...and this is home.

Fullness!

About the Author

MINISTRY

Rick is a spiritual motivator, event speaker, and a mentor and advisor to many Christian leaders. Countless lives have been transformed as he has preached and taught thousands of speaking engagements.

Using personal examples of faith adventures, self-effacing humor, and a clear lifestyle example, Rick leads and encourages people to experience the Kingdom of Heaven in this life. His message is that God has given us all we need in Jesus Christ, and if we believe, we can enjoy every bit of it.

Because, Rick has an ability to relate to all types of people, he is invited to many different kinds of groups, churches and organizations.

LIFESTYLE

A youthful, vibrant 50-something that hasn't had a cold, flu or headache since 1982, Rick walks in divine health, and believes he will never be sick again.

The Lord has blessed Rick with prosperity and success as a minister, businessman, and family man.

HISTORY, BACKGROUND & EXPERIENCE

- Saved from a life of drugs, alcohol abuse and crime in 1979 at the age of 21.
- Attended Rhema Bible Training Center in '83-'84.
- Associate Pastor '84-'88.
- Pastor '89-'98.
- Itinerant Speaker '98-present.

To contact Rick Manis Ministries
Please write or call:

PO Box 784327
Winter Garden FL 34778
877-407-9331

Or visit us on the web at:
Rickmanis.com

Or email us at:
info@rickmanis.com

Other books by Rick Manis:

The Now Zone

Glory in the Glass

Get them at Amazon.com or Rickmanis.com

You may also be interested in:

"Heaven on Earth University"

This Life Mastery Course is an audio curriculum you can study at your own pace.

Learn to master the human experience with this interactive study system that deals with every area of life.

The curriculum includes:
- 18 lessons
- 8 CDs
- DVD
- Workbook
- Graduate Certificate

All for $50!

Contact the ministry or go to rickmanis.com

Made in the USA
Charleston, SC
08 July 2014